HELICOPTERS

MARK DARTFORD

angus

This edition published in 2004 by Angus Books
12 Ravensbury Terrace
London
SW18 4RL

ISBN 1-904594-37-9

The Brown Reference Group plc
8 Chapel Place
Rivington Street
London
EC2A 3DQ

Production by Omnipress,
Eastbourne, UK
Printed and bound in Dubai

This book uses black and yellow chevrons as a decorative element on some headers. They do not point to other elements on the page.

Contents

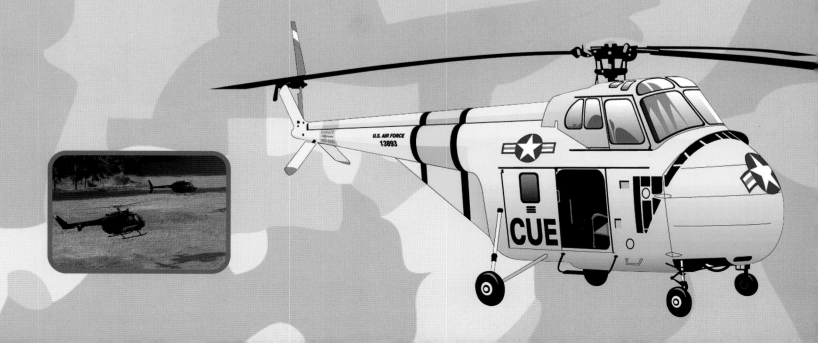

Introduction

The oncoming sound of spinning rotor blades fills the evening air. Soon a dozen black dots, low on the skyline, grow bigger as the helicopters approach. Suddenly a stream of rockets and machine-gun fire streaks across the tops of the trees, causing panic and destruction below. The helicopter—slow and squat compared to fixed-wing strike aeroplanes—is still a powerful weapon.

INCOMING

Bell UH1 Hueys swoop down on a low-level mission in Vietnam during the 1960s.

>> **autogiro** = an aircraft that has both a propeller and a rotor blade

Art, Science, and Aviation

The idea of using a rotating wing to lift a person-carrying capsule off the ground is not new. The Italian artist and inventor Leonardo da Vinci came up with a design in the 1490s. Many people believe that his designs for a flying machine were hundreds of years ahead of their time. In fact, it was not until the 1920s that a true rotorcraft successfully lifted off.

FIRST FLIGHTS

A Spaniard named Don Juan de la Cierva built and flew the first successful **autogiro** in the 1920s. It was a small aircraft that used a propeller-driven motor to provide forward speed. It also had a free-spinning rotor to give **lift.** A decade later, Germany's Fw61 appeared. It was the first pilot-controlled rotorcraft.

DA VINCI'S DESIGN

Da Vinci's plan used an upward-facing airscrew. His design was never built.

GERMAN SUCCESS

The Focke-Achgelis was a helicopter flown from the deck of a World War II (1939–1945) submarine.

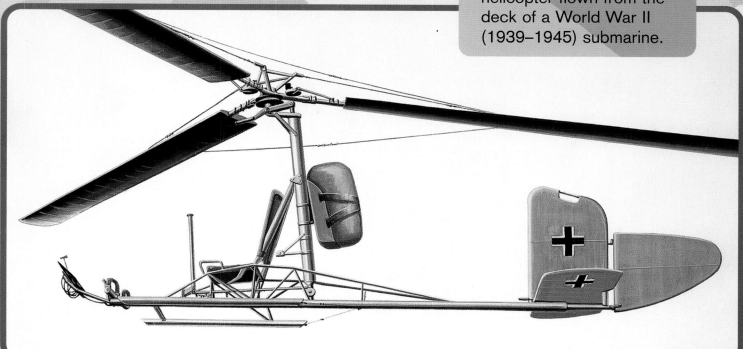

Sikorsky

In the United States, Igor Sikorsky developed the first military helicopter that could be made in large numbers. It had a single main rotor and a small **anti-torque tail rotor**.

HOVERFLY

The Sikorsky R4 was the only mass-produced military helicopter of World War II.

Korea

The helicopter made its real combat start in Korea in the early 1950s. It mostly carried supplies and wounded personnel to and from the battle zones.

EXPLOSIVE LOAD

An HRS Sikorsky helicopter hovers as marines load weapons into its cargo net in Korea.

>> **anti-torque tail rotor** – the rotor that stops a helicopter spinning around

Late 1900s

Helicopter (chopper) warfare came into its own during the Vietnam War (roughly 1965–1975). Vietnam is a mountainous country, and much of it is covered in jungle. U.S. forces used helicopters for active combat missions and all kinds of transport and supply.

DO-ALL

A wounded soldier is carried from an Iroquois UH1 helicopter during the Vietnam War.

PEACEKEEPING

Helicopters played an increasingly important part in conflicts of the late 1900s. These included the war in Bosnia (1980s) and **Operation Desert Storm** (1991). Choppers were also part of operations against terrorists in Afghanistan in 2001 and 2002.

DESERT STORM

A U.S. Army MH53 Stallion stirs up the sand in Iraq during Operation Desert Storm.

>> **Operation Desert Storm** – a 1991 war against Iraq after it invaded Kuwait

The Rotorcraft Role

Modern helicopters come in all shapes and sizes. They perform many roles. Anti-armour helicopters work on the front line, taking out enemy tanks and guns. At sea, helicopters are used for information gathering, antisubmarine warfare and air/sea rescues. Large helicopters transport troops, equipment and supplies.

TANK BUSTER

The AH1 Cobra is a proven attack helicopter. It is equipped with tube-launched TOW missiles. It carries out short-range, low-level strikes against individual enemy targets such as tanks. Cobras destroyed more than 200 tanks and armoured fighting vehicles during Operation Desert Storm.

Helicopters at Sea

Helicopters make ideal ship-borne aircraft. They can take off and land using a small area. They are easier to store than fixed-wing aircraft. A helicopter can hover steadily in one place, even in high winds.

ABOVE AND BELOW THE WAVES

A Canadian Sea King prepares to drop a **sonar buoy** into the ocean, to listen for underwater intruders. Anti-submarine warfare (ASW) helicopters are not just passive observers. They can also drop mines and **depth charges** on enemy submarines.

FIRST UP, LAST DOWN

Every U.S. aircraft carrier has a rescue helicopter. It stands by to pick up crewmembers if an aeroplane misses the landing deck. This SH3 Sea King helicopter is the first up during missions or exercises and is the last to land.

>> **depth charge** = an underwater bomb triggered by water pressure

Heavy Lifters

Large helicopters carry out transport duties. They can deliver combat personnel and equipment close to the battlefront, without the need for a runway or airport.

ANYTHING, ANYWHERE

A CH54 Sky Crane helicopter prepares to lift a cargo container during the Vietnam War.

CHINOOK

The twin-rotor UH47 Chinook is a versatile transport helicopter with a large cargo area. It can land up to fourteen fully equipped combat troops in a small forest clearing.

>> **covert operations** = undercover missions, usually behind enemy lines

Coast Guard

The U.S. Coast Guard uses helicopters to patrol the U.S. coastline. The Coast Guard's job is to protect the shores and to assist people in distress.

SECURITY AT SEA

A Coast Guard HH60 Jayhawk patrols the ocean. The Jayhawk is a medium-range recovery helicopter, here fitted with an external stretcher.

SPECIAL OPERATIONS

Military helicopters have an important job in **covert operations**. They perform combat search-and-rescue (SAR) missions, resupply troops and land army **Special Forces** behind enemy lines.

PAVE HAWK

An HH60 Pave Hawk pararescue helicopter contacts Special Forces behind enemy lines. The Pave Hawk can reach remote locations at night or in rough weather. It has a refuelling probe for long-range operations.

Helicopter Missions

Helicopters can fly in rough weather and can land and take off using small spaces. They are ideal for rescue work and special operations. During the Korean War, helicopters found and flew the wounded to field hospitals. In the early 2000s, helicopters searched the mountains of Afghanistan for terrorists. Over time, the helicopter has proved to be a vital part of the military's hardware.

BOSNIA

In 1996 U.S. forces used UH60 helicopters to put combat personnel into enemy areas in the forests of Bosnia.

>> **evacuation** = removing wounded personnel from the battle zone

Field Hospitals

There was a shortage of helicopters during the Korean War. Their use for medical **evacuation** evolved over time. Some of the remote battle zones were up to 40 miles or more from the nearest Mobile Army Surgical Hospital (MASH). Helicopters provided a quick and smooth transit from battlefield to the hospital. They saved many lives that might otherwise have been lost had wounded been transported overland.

AIR AID

A wounded U.S. 21st Infantry soldier is lifted onto a helicopter for evacuation to a hospital in Korea, April 1951. Communist North Korea invaded South Korea in 1950 but retreated after UN forces stepped in.

CASEVAC CHOPPER

An 8225th MASH **casevac** helicopter team in Korea in October 1951. It has a full set of life-saving equipment to help the wounded.

>> **casevac** – military abbreviation for Casualty Evacuation

13

Civilians in Distress

Helicopters often take part in civilian rescue operations. They can hover in bad weather over rough seas to pick up shipwrecked sailors or land in small mountain clearings to rescue lost climbers. Organizations like the U.S. Coast Guard, Air National Guard and local rescue units save many lives.

UNLUCKY DAY

Saturday, January 13, 2001, was an unlucky day for a 14-year old mountain biker from California. The young man was separated from his brother in the Angeles National Forest. The Ventura County Search-and-Rescue helicopter was alerted, and a team flew out to find him. They found him alive and well after 48 hours in the open and airlifted him to safety.

SHIPWRECK RESCUE

A U.S. Coast Guard HH60 helicopter hovers above the deck of the passenger liner *Sea Breeze I*. In December 2000, the 600-foot ship was **foundering** in the Atlantic Ocean 300 miles off the coast of Virginia. The Coast Guard sent two HH60 search-and-rescue helicopters and two C130 Hercules aeroplanes to the scene. In heavy seas and high winds, 34 crewmembers were **winched** to safety before the ship finally sank.

LONG JOB

"... Finally, with a menacing cargo boom just five feet away from the helicopter's rotor blades, the pararescue man was lowered aboard the ship. It was ten minutes short of midnight. We had been on an alert since noon that day and now, almost 12 hours later, work was just beginning...."

Major James E. McArdle Jr, U.S. Air Force Rescue and Recovery Squadron, Korea

ON THE WAY

Pararescue specialists from an Air National Guard HH60 Pave Hawk use a rope ladder to rescue a swimmer near the Golden Gate Bridge in San Francisco Bay.

>> **winched** = lifted up to a helicopter by a motorized cable and harness

15

Long-Distance Recovery

Conflicts that affect the rest of the world can occur almost anywhere. So international peacekeeping forces have to operate at long distances. Aeroplanes and helicopters make such missions possible.

BOSNIA RESCUE

U.S. Air Force pilot Captain Scott O'Grady arrives at a U.S. airbase in Italy after his rescue. His F16 fighter jet was shot down on a UN mission over Bosnia in June 1995. A rescue operation was launched from the USS *Kearsarge*, using marine CH53 helicopters. After a week of avoiding enemy search parties, Captain O'Grady was finally located and flown back to safety.

53S STANDBY

Sea Stallion helicopters sit on the deck of USS *Kearsarge* in the Adriatic Sea.

HEROES

"The people I want to thank ... are the men and women of the Navy and Marine Corps ... who came in there and saved me. If you want to find heroes, that's where to look."

Captain Scott O'Grady,
U.S. Air Force, June 1995

Enduring Freedom

Coalition helicopters were a vital factor in securing safe operating bases in Afghanistan in 2001 and 2002. Their arrival was just the beginning of a long international war against terrorism.

OPERATION ANACONDA

In May 2002, a ground crew unloaded a UH60 Black Hawk from a C17 Globemaster transport aeroplane. The operation to enclose and destroy **al-Qaeda** forces in Afghanistan would not have been possible without the support of both attack and transport helicopters.

Helicopter Skills

Fighting helicopters have very different characteristics from fixed-wing aeroplanes. They are slower but they can hover and even fly backwards. The pilots engaged in helicopter warfare make effective use of such differences.

STRINGS ATTACHED

Troops **rappel** down ropes from a UH1 Huey.

VTOL

Vertical takeoff and landing (VTOL) gives the helicopter its edge. VTOL sets helicopters apart from most fixed-wing aircraft. The ability to hover in the air makes the helicopter ideal for covert and **reconnaissance** operations. A military helicopter often acts halfway between a combat aircraft and an armoured fighting vehicle.

AEROBATIC

A French-built Aerospatiale Super Puma avoids contact with the enemy. Modern strike helicopters must be extremely easy to fly to avoid enemy missile fire.

HIDDEN THREAT

The Apache AH64 was designed to hide behind ground features. It can then pop up and fire its anti-tank missiles, before dropping down out of sight again. Ground features, such as forests, also absorb engine noise.

INVISIBLE ABOVE THE WAVES

A Seahawk lowers a sonar buoy into the sea. Hovering above the ocean, U.S. Navy ASW helicopters cannot be found by submarines.

Formations

Many rescue and attack missions are carried out using several helicopters together. This **tactic** increases the chance of success but also provides more **covering fire.** Sometimes, a "stand-off" helicopter is also added. It flies above and to one side of the group, acting as an airborne guardian.

OUTASIGHT

A German army Bell Jet Ranger leads, with an MBB105 light reconnaissance helicopter (*bottom*) as wingman. They are on ground-hugging combat air patrol (CAP).

TWO'S COMPANY

Helicopters frequently fly missions in pairs or combinations of pairs, with a leader and a wingman for cover. This basic formation is also used by fixed-wing aircraft.

Racetracks and Dogbones

A standard tactic is the L-attack. This involves a string of helicopters in an angled approach, intended to confuse enemy fire. The L-attack then develops into either a "dogbone" or "racetrack" pattern. With correct spacing, the helicopters can almost continuously shoot at the target. The dogbone allows an even spread of gunfire from each side of the aircraft. The racetrack keeps just one side facing the enemy, if only one side-gun is fitted.

SAFETY IN NUMBERS

A string of Pave Hawk helicopters approaches its target over mountainous terrain.

SLASHING ATTACK

"The L-attack is used for a slashing attack. The idea is that either en route to an insertion point or en route to a survivor you would encounter some opposition."

Lieutenant Commander J. Nordhill, U.S. Navy Helicopter Combat Support Squadron

Helicopter Parade

There are many different kinds of helicopters. Some are lightweight, **single-seat** reconnaissance and observation aircraft. Long-distance big lifters are also popular. Anti-submarine and anti-armour strike helicopters have recently joined the parade.

AH1 SUPER COBRA

The Super Cobra is a legend. It was first manufactured by Bell Helicopters, Inc., in 1966. The AH1 logged more than 1 million combat flying hours in Vietnam. The helicopter has seen more than thirty years of continuous development since that time.

Details:
Crew: 2
Length: 45 ft. 3 in.
Width: 10 ft. 9 in.
Propulsion: 2 x 1,690 hp **turboshaft** engines
Max Speed: 175 mph
Ceiling: 14,750 ft.
Armament: 1 x 20mm cannons, various missiles, rockets

SH60 SEA HAWK

The U.S. Army has the MH/UH53 Black Hawk. The Sea Hawk is the U.S. Navy's carrier-borne, anti-submarine, and search-and-rescue aircraft. It also carries cargo, is involved in special operations, and takes on radar reconnaissance tasks.

Details:
Crew: 3
Length: 50 ft
Width: 5 ft 6 in.
Propulsion: 2 x 1,662 hp turboshaft engines
Max Speed: 175 mph
Ceiling: 13,000 ft.
Armament: 2 x torpedoes, 1 x Penguin anti-ship missile

CH47 CHINOOK

The Chinook is a twin-engine, twin-rotor helicopter. It is designed for transporting troops, cargo and weapons in all weather conditions. Development first began in 1961. The aircraft has been regularly upgraded since then.

Details:
Crew: 2
Length: 50 ft.
Width: 14 ft 9 in.
Propulsion: 2 x 1770 hp turboshaft engines
Max Speed: 167 mph
Ceiling: 10,000 ft.
Armament: 4,000 lb. external load

>> **turboshaft** = a rotor shaft driven by a jet engine with turbine blades

Helicopter Parade

DEFENDER 500

Boeing/McDonnell Douglas in the United States developed the Defender 500 to sell to foreign military forces. Many versions are available, including anti-tank, combat air support and observation models.

Details:
Crew: 1–2
Length: 24 ft. 10 in.
Width: 6 ft. 3 in.
Propulsion: 1 x 375 hp turboshaft engine
Max Speed: 150 mph
Ceiling: 15,000 ft.
Armament: 2 x 7.62mm machine guns, Hydra rockets, Hellfire/TOW/Stinger missiles, grenade launchers

ROOIVALK CSH2 COMBAT HELICOPTER

The Rooivalk was developed by South Africa in 1998. It is equipped with air-to-air missiles, anti-tank missiles and a rapid-fire cannon. It is designed to be hard to pick up on radar and has high resistance to damage.

Details:
Crew: 2
Length: 61 ft. 3 in.
Width: 10 ft.
Propulsion: 2 x 1845 hp turboshaft engines
Max Speed: 193 mph
Ceiling: 20,000 ft.
Armament: 1 x 20mm cannon, Mokopa anti-tank missiles, Mistral or Denel air-to-air missiles, **unguided rockets**

>> **unguided rocket** = a rocket that has no onboard guidance or control system

MI24 HIND

The MI24 Hind is built in Russia. It is a combined combat-assault helicopter and helicopter-gunship. It was used extensively during the Soviet Union's war in Afghanistan in the 1980s.

Details:
Crew: 2
Length: 57 ft. 5 in.
Width: 10 ft.
Propulsion: 2 x 2,200 hp **turbines**
Max Speed: 168 mph
Ceiling: 15,000 ft.
Armament: 1 x 12.7mm machine gun, 1 x 30mm cannon, anti-tank guided missiles, rockets, 2,200 lb. bomb load

>> **turbine** – a jet engine with turbine blades to increase power output

Helicopter Parade

MH60 PAVE HAWK

The Sikorsky MH60 Pave Hawk is a twin-engine medium-lift helicopter operated by the U.S. Air Force Special Operations Command. Its main jobs are transporting Special Forces troops and conducting combat search-and-rescue missions. MH60s played a major part in Operation Desert Storm in 1991 and in Afghanistan in 2001 and 2002.

Details:
Crew: 4
Length: 64 ft. 8 in.
Width: 5 ft. 6 in.
Propulsion: 2 x 1630 hp T700 turboshaft engines
Max Speed: 184 mph
Ceiling: 19,000 ft.
Armament: 2 x 7.62mm miniguns

SA341 GAZELLE

The Gazelle is a French-built **light utility** helicopter. It can be adapted for anti-tank and anti-helicopter tasks, as well as light transport and training. It is used by more than 20 countries worldwide.

Details:
Crew: 1–2
Length: 31 ft. 3 in.
Width: 6 ft. 6 in.
Propulsion: 1 x 590 hp turboshaft engine
Max Speed: 193 mph
Ceiling: 16,000 ft.
Armament: 7.62mm machine guns and/or 20mm cannon, anti-tank and anti-aircraft missiles, rockets

AS565 PANTHER/DAUPHIN

The Panther is a military version of France's Aerospatiale Dauphin. It is used by many countries, including the U.S. Coast Guard.

Details:
Crew: 2–3
Length: 37 ft. 6 in.
Width: 7 ft. 6 in.
Propulsion: 2 x **Turbomeca** turboshaft engines
Max Speed: 170 mph
Ceiling: 10,200 ft.
Armament: rockets, anti-tank missiles

>> **Turbomeca** – a manufacturer of helicopter jet engines based in France

Future Helicopters

The next generation of helicopters and VTOL aircraft will have greater stealth and more **avionics.** They will not require as much maintenance time.

COMANCHE

The Boeing–Sikorsky RAH66 is the U.S. Army's armed reconnaissance helicopter for the next generation. It will replace the AH1 Super Cobra and OH58 Warrior reconnaissance helicopters and will supplement the AH64 Apache.

FASTER, MEANER, LEANER

The Comanche will have more powerful motors than the Apache or Warrior. It will be able to carry more missiles and will be harder to find either on radar or by eye.

Tilt-rotor Technology

Aircraft manufacturers have been experimenting with **tilt-rotor aeroplanes** for several decades. The advantage lies in being able to combine the best of both fixed-wing aircraft and VTOL aircraft. Despite setbacks, the tilt-rotor aircraft is probably the future for military medium transport.

OSPREY

The V22 Osprey is an experimental tilt-rotor slated to replace the Vietnam-era transport helicopters of the U.S. Marine Corps. The Osprey can fly like a normal aeroplane. It can also land and take off from a small platform or unpaved area.

ROTOR X-CRAFT

An experimental tilt-rotor prototype

STOP-GO STORY

After several fatal accidents during trials, the V22 project was put on hold in 2000. In May 2002, however, tests resumed. The motors can rotate, pointing upward for vertical operation and forward for horizontal flight.

tilt-rotor aeroplane – an aircraft with propellers that can also be rotors

Future Helicopters

Reducing the number of mechanical parts is an important part of future helicopter design. This will reduce wear and tear and high maintenance costs. Replacing the tail anti-torque rotor with something simpler is one solution.

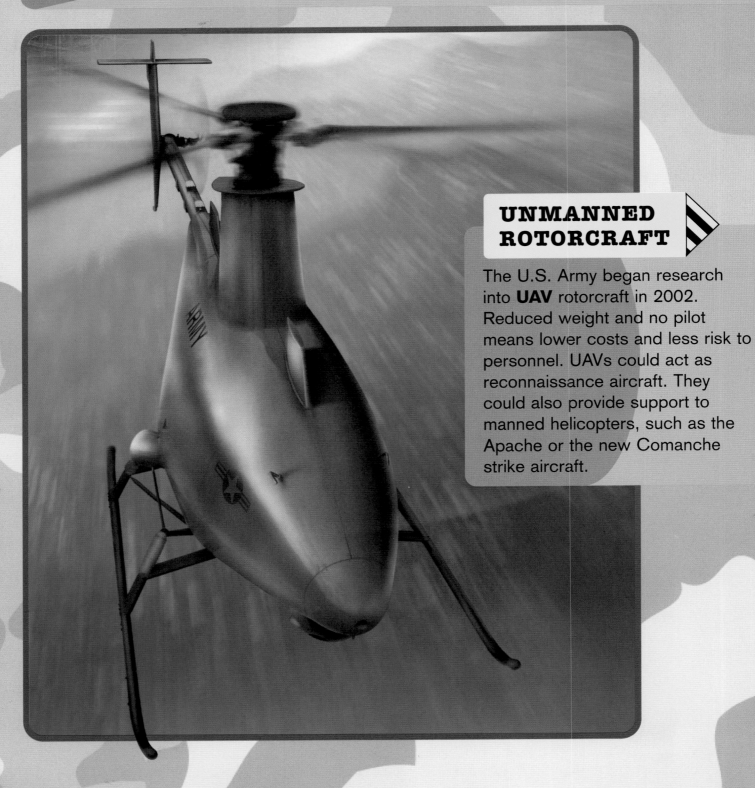

UNMANNED ROTORCRAFT

The U.S. Army began research into **UAV** rotorcraft in 2002. Reduced weight and no pilot means lower costs and less risk to personnel. UAVs could act as reconnaissance aircraft. They could also provide support to manned helicopters, such as the Apache or the new Comanche strike aircraft.

HUMMINGBIRD

The A160 Hummingbird is an unmanned **surveillance** and targeting rotorcraft project. The lightweight vehicle will remain airborne for up to 48 hours without refuelling.

Nose section can be changed to make room for different types of equipment

Control aerial

Foldable landing gear with 33-inch ground clearance to allow space for extra aerials or other items

AIR SCOOTER

This experimental one-person heliscooter has attracted some military interest. It could provide combat troops with extra mobility. The aircraft has fan rotors that can be tilted to change direction, with a handgrip throttle to control speed and lift.

Index

Picture Sources